A Day in the Life of a Marine Biologist

A Day in the Life of a
Marine Biologist

WILLIAM JASPERSOHN

Little, Brown and Company

BOSTON   TORONTO

Books by William Jaspersohn

A DAY IN THE LIFE OF A VETERINARIAN

HOW THE FOREST GREW

THE BALLPARK
One Day Behind the Scenes at a Major League Game

A DAY IN THE LIFE OF A TELEVISION NEWS REPORTER

A DAY IN THE LIFE OF A MARINE BIOLOGIST

FIRST EDITION

Photography credits: page 70, lower left by Douglas R. Herr; page 70, upper left and lower right by Alan Poole; page 65, right by Russell Hill. All other photographs by William Jaspersohn.

Library of Congress Cataloging in Publication Data

Jaspersohn, William.
  A day in the life of a marine biologist.

  Summary: Follows a day in the life of marine biologist Dr. Arthur Humes, who has discovered new ocean animals in Earth's major bodies of water.
  1. Marine biologists—Vocational guidance— Juvenile literature. 2. Humes, Arthur Grover, 1916– —Juvenile literature. 3. Marine biologists—Massachusetts—Biography—Juvenile literature. [1. Marine biologists—Vocational guidance. 2. Vocational guidance. 3. Humes, Arthur Grover, 1916–   ] I. Title.
  QH91.45.J37   574.92′092′4   [B]   81–20721
  ISBN 0–316–45814–7   AACR2

MU

Published simultaneously in Canada
by Little, Brown & Company (Canada) Limited

PRINTED IN THE UNITED STATES OF AMERICA

This Book is for
Andrew Godfrey with love

You know how it is when you see an unusual tree or flower or bird: you want to know it, you want its name. Naming is the start of knowing. That is how it was for Arthur Humes and seashells. As a little boy he used to walk the narrow beaches of Falmouth, Massachusetts, on Cape Cod, and find shells. Times seemed simpler then. Horse-drawn ice wagons clattered up the steep streets of Falmouth Heights where Arthur's family summered; ladies wore floppy sexless garments called bathing costumes when they swam; men strolled the sidewalks in straw boater hats or felt derbies and dark, wrinkled suits; lawn parties at the great houses on the Heights wafted scraps of jazz and laughter on the summer air. It was 1925. Arthur, nine, collected shells. The sea lapped the shore, the sun felt good on his back. He collected. When he had enough shells he boxed them and took them to Boston, rode the trolley to the Boston Society of Natural History which then had a kindly man named Charles W. Johnson on the staff.

"Sure I'll help you," said Johnson when he saw the shells. His moustache was neatly clipped, his smile was broad; his bald head gleamed under the wash of cool light from his office windows. "Sure I'll help you." He identified every one of Arthur's shells and when he was done he reached in a drawer in his desk and said, "Here, keep these, too," and dropped shells from his own collection in Arthur's hand.

That was the start of it. Barefoot and in knickers Arthur combed the beaches, rocks, and tidepools around Falmouth, finding shells, shells. He borrowed shell identification books from the library. The Latin names enchanted him. It was a time when schools still taught Latin and Greek. But always, always the first passion was the shells, how beautiful they were, each one different: rough, smooth, chalky, whorled, chambered, speckled, hard, soft, brittle, translucent like his own toenails or bits of chipped milky glass. A shell was an animal's house, its armor. And there were so many different kinds, the sea kept tossing them up; the wonderful sea; life was so abundant. Arthur labeled his shells and put them in paper trays and touched them and dreamed of owning one of every kind of seashell in the world.

He still owns those shells. They rest in their paper trays in a gumwood cabinet in the basement of his house in Falmouth, Massachusetts. Each shell is labeled, in place, in a gumwood box his father, a businessman, bought for young Arthur a half century ago. Arthur no longer collects shells. A person grows up, his tastes change, he tries to find the work that suits him, he changes.

But Arthur Humes hasn't changed, inside he hasn't. He still collects, though not shells. He still searches and names. He finds animals in the oceans, tiny ones, unknown to others before he found them, and since they have no names he gives them one. His work today is an outgrowth of his passion as a boy. For a living he does what he loves. He looks at life in the sea and names it.

He is a marine biologist, a person who studies the science of ocean life. His specialty, *taxonomy*, is the naming and ordering of living forms, life classification. As a marine taxonomist he discovers new ocean animals, gives them names, and determines their places in the animal kingdom. And new animals are out there, waiting to be discovered. Arthur found new animals in the Pacific Ocean. He found some in the Irish Sea. He found some in the Indian Ocean, the Atlantic Ocean, the Philippine Sea, the Mozambique Channel, the Gulf of Mexico. It was just like hunting for shells, only the scale was vaster; the world was his beach. He rode freighters to Africa and Borneo. His microscopes accompanied him in padded black chests. With air tanks strapped to his back and rubber fins on his feet and a swim mask pressed to his face he once dove to a depth of one hundred sixty-five feet in the blue waters off Madagascar in search of animals, ocean fleas, that he guessed might live among corals. The water pressure at that depth was tremendous. The ocean squeezed his body like a giant invisible hand. And yet he felt weightless. It was wonderful. Never had work been so much fun!

For thirty years Arthur Humes has combed the seas for specimens. He is something of a legend in his field. Hundreds of scientific papers have flowed from his pen. He has taught some three thousand students. He remembers buying them lobsters to study, from fish vendors around Boston. For the past eleven years he has directed a graduate program for marine biologists called BUMP, short for Boston University Marine Program. BUMP is headquartered on the campus of the Marine Biological Laboratory in Woods Hole, Massachusetts. The setting is perfect for a marine biologist. There are laboratories with running seawater. There are computers and libraries and aquariums. The Woods Hole Oceanographic Institution is just down the block, as is the sea and a fleet of seagoing research ships.

Arthur Humes's day as a marine biologist begins at dawn with grapefruit juice and cereal. An hour later, briefcase in hand, he walks from his house and down the sunken flagstone path to his car. His step is quick. His briefcase contains his lunch. The drive to his office is pleasant, down a street lined with soaring oaks and white picket fences and homes with blue shutters and weathered shakes. Within minutes a harbor slips into view. Boats bob on their moorings, scattering sheets of brilliant sunlight over the water. The island of Martha's Vineyard floats cakelike, tan and green, four miles distant. Arthur smiles.

He parks his car in a lot beside Eel Pond, the harbor across from his building. A student pedaling by on a bicycle shouts, "Hi, Dr. Humes!" And it's true, he is a doctor, though not one who practices medicine. He is a Doctor of Philosophy, or Ph.D., in Marine Biology. To earn that doctorate degree he studied four years as an undergraduate at Brown University and another four as a graduate student at Louisiana State University and the University of Illinois. Now, you don't *have* to get a doctorate degree to work in marine biology — you can be a lab technician with only a high school diploma. But if you want a university post — and most marine biologists teach — and if you want your research work recognized by other scientists, then a Ph.D. is essential. Arthur Humes is quite emphatic on the subject. "Get a broad scientific background as an undergraduate," he says. "Take physics, mathematics, chemistry, biology, then shoot for the top. Marine biology is a field with fewer and fewer positions, and a doctorate's required for most of them."

Arthur enters his building. Cypress planking sheathes its sides. The building is named after the famous marine biologist Jacques Loeb, a German who lived in Woods Hole at the end of the nineteenth century and who did pioneering work in physiology, which is the study of animals' bodies and how they function. Pictures of Loeb in the Marine Biological Laboratory archives show a short, powerful-looking man with a steady gaze and a thick dark moustache. Arthur says that Loeb is still an inspiration to marine biologists because he always did his scientific work *objectively*, that is, with an open mind. "As a scientist," says Arthur, "it's important not to be biased, but instead to draw your conclusions from proven fact."

There is always paperwork awaiting Arthur when he arrives in his office. Bills must be paid, students' papers read. Autumn is an especially busy time because that's when applications for next year's batch of BUMP students must be reviewed. Altogether, Arthur and his staff of four faculty members sift through some two hundred applications each year from young people wanting to become marine biologists. All the applicants have undergraduate degrees, and most are qualified, but only about eight new students each year can be picked.

At 8:30 A.M. BUMP's secretary, Dorothy Hahn, arrives for work. Arthur leaves some letters for her to type. And then at 8:55 he gathers a crisp sheaf of notes off his desk and heads downstairs to teach a class. He feels alert. His thoughts are focused. It's going to be an interesting day. A field trip is planned for Arthur and his class of first-year students. At 11 A.M. a ship will transport them to an island several miles from Woods Hole. The tides are right. The skies are clear. But since the students will be collecting examples of the many kinds of marine creatures that live on the island, Arthur first must brief them on where and how to collect.

It's a good group of students, men and women, all in their first year at BUMP. Each went to a different undergraduate college, and each has a different reason for wanting to become a marine biologist, but all have certain qualities in common. They all love biology. They all love the sea. Each in some way wants to do something that will benefit life on this planet.

Arthur's course is teaching the students about the *invertebrate* marine animals around Cape Cod, that is, animals without any backbones. The course is entitled "Marine Invertebrate Zoology," and it's a necessary subject for anyone becoming a marine biologist.

The other teacher today is Dr. Sidney Tamm, who trained at the University of Chicago. His specialty is the study of one-celled animals and how they move.

His class of undergraduates from Boston University has come to hear Arthur's lecture, too. They are seniors, down from BU for the fall term, taking a special course with BUMP professors on different aspects of marine science.

Helping Sid Tamm and Arthur with the courses are two assistants, or *teaching fellows* as they're called, Tom Duncan and Mas Dojiri. Their job is to assist on field trips and supervise the classes during laboratory sessions, and occasionally teach the classes themselves. Both are older BUMP students — well, Tom *was* a BUMP student. He just earned his Ph.D. this summer.

Now Arthur begins his lecture. His enthusiasm is real. Many invertebrate marine animals, he explains, live in *intertidal zones*, which are areas of the seashore covered with water at high tide but exposed at low tide. There are five major kinds of intertidal zones, he continues. They include:

1) rocky intertidal zones,
2) marshes,
3) mud flats,
4) sandy intertidal zones, or beaches, and
5) salt ponds.

"Now, on today's field trip to the island," says Arthur, "we will sample zones one through four on this list." He then describes the kinds of animals found in each zone. Burrowing animals, for example, such as worms, tend to live on sandy or muddy shores, he explains, while animals that need something to attach themselves to, such as mussels, tend to live on rocks. But, he emphasizes, all shore invertebrates are affected by:

1) temperature changes,
2) exposure to sunlight,
3) food availability,
4) water loss, or desiccation,
5) the saltiness, or *salinity*, of the water,
6) the amount of living space in the zone, and
7) man.

"Number seven should come as no surprise," says Arthur. "Man's the worst enemy these animals have. Let's remember to exercise restraint as we do our collecting today. We don't need fifty thousand specimens. Please be good scientists and take only one or two of each animal you find."

The class members nod that they will. Arthur smiles. Then he glances at the clock and says, "Our ship leaves for the island in forty-five minutes. Any questions?" Nobody raises a hand. "Okay then," says Arthur, "let's get ready for the field trip."

The ship they will be taking is the R.V. (which stands for "Research Vessel") *Ciona*, owned by the Marine Biological Laboratory and rented to Arthur and his students for field trips. She's a sturdy vessel, forty feet long, and she's docked now in Eel Pond, fueled and ready for the island trip.

Meanwhile, out behind the BUMP offices, Mas and Tom supervise distribution of the collecting gear. They hand the students dipnets. They hand them buckets. They hand them box sieves, shovels, forks, jars, bait seines, bottles, spades, clamforks — everything they'll need for collecting specimens in the field.

A few minutes before departure students and teachers assemble at the dock. The students are quiet. They wait to be told what to do. Some decide to pull on their boots now. Others simply stand. Many sport colorful nylon packs containing food, and yellow slickers in case of storms. Finally a signal is given and everyone boards the ship. Talk comes easier now. Tension about leaving turns to relief. The collecting gear is stowed behind the wheelhouse. The captain at the helm, "Brud" Lane, twists the ignition key in its lock and with a soft rumble the *Ciona*'s big diesel engine thrums to life. Tight fists of blue smoke pump from the white stack. Nobody moves. Captain Lane reverses the ship until the snapline goes slack and Tom Duncan can lift it off its mooring. "Line clear!" shouts Tom. Captain Lane nods and shifts the *Ciona*'s gears into forward. The ship gives a lurch. "Here we go!" somebody whispers, and the ship glides smoothly from the dock.

Honnn-k! Honk! Honk!

Captain Lane gives the *Ciona*'s horn three sharp blasts.

In his hut above Eel Pond the drawbridge man hears the ship's bleat and punches a button on his control panel marked STOP LIGHT–TRAF. This activates the bridge's red light, stopping traffic on the street. Down on the pond, meanwhile, the *Ciona* patiently idles. The drawbridge man next steps out on the bridge and shuts the iron gates, then returns to the hut and presses two buttons: PUMP ON and RAISE BRIDGE. From under the bridge comes a whooping mechanical whine, and slowly, almost impossibly, the bridge begins to rise on its hydraulic lifts. When finally it can rise no more, the drawbridge man presses a fourth button, PONDSIDE GO, which gives the pondside *Ciona* the green light. Then and only then does the *Ciona* pass under the bridge.

A minute later she is steering toward open seas.

Since it's almost noon now, Arthur and his students eat their lunches on the *Ciona*'s main deck. The seas are calm. Woods Hole slips quickly from view.

A half hour later a student points off the port rail and asks, "Is that it?"

On the horizon an island has popped into view.

"That's it," says Arthur. The sight of the island stirs him deeply.

"Okay, if I can have your attention," he says to the students as the *Ciona* glides quietly into the island's harbor. "As some of you may know, this island is privately owned. Now, its owner has asked that we not smoke or start fires or light matches while we're here for the simple reason that there's no firefighting equipment on the island. Aside from that let's, as always, do our work well and not abuse the privilege of being here."

With that the *Ciona* docks at the island pier and everyone disembarks. Minutes later, equipment in hand, the group hikes up a wooded road that runs through the heart of the island and leads to the collection site.

The site is a sheltered cove, which, as Arthur says, contains so many different intertidal zones — mud, rock, sand, marsh — that it's perfect for finding specimens.

The site is reached by crossing a fine old stone bridge at the cove's narrowest end, then clambering down a rocky embankment.

Since collecting specimens is a wet and sometimes dirty business, Arthur recommends that students wear a good pair of hip waders when they go into intertidal zones.

Now he divides the classes into teams of three and four, and the teams divide the tools, and everyone fans out along the shore and goes to work.

The first zone the classes sample is an area of the cove where the bottom is pebbly mud. The best way of sampling such a zone is with a spade and a simple sifting device called a *box sieve*. Arthur says that anyone can construct a box sieve by knocking the bottom off a wooden bottle crate and replacing it with a piece of medium- or fine-gauge wire mesh. The students use box sieves that Arthur built.

When a spadeful of mud from the cove bottom is dropped onto the mesh and the box is shaken in the water, the sediment drops through the mesh, leaving the animals.

And the first spadefuls of mud bring up some fine specimens. There is a clam. But what kind of clam, specifically? New Englanders would say it's a quahog, while Southerners would call it either a round or a hard-shelled clam. And fish market people would say it's a littleneck, cherrystone, or chowder clam depending on its size. These are a clam's *common names*. Which one does a marine biologist use? Answer: none of them.

Instead, scientists worldwide have a system of classifying animals and plants that avoids this confusion of names. Using words from Latin and Greek, the system classifies animals within seven categories: *kingdom, phylum, class, order, family, genus,* and *species*. The categories "kingdom" through "family" serve to place animals into smaller and more closely related groups until finally "genus" and "species" describe only one particular type animal. Together, "genus" and "species" form an animal's *scientific name*, and it is this name that marine biologists use instead of common ones.

Most scientific names have a story behind them. For example, because quahog shells were once used by Indians as money, or wampum, the scientist who named this clam called it *Mercenaria mercenaria* (mer-sin-AIR-ee-uh mer-sin-AIR-ee-uh), which in Latin means "one who uses itself for money." And this lugworm is scientifically known as *Arenicola cristata* (are-uh-NIK-o-la cris-TA-ta), or "crested one that burrows in sand." Good marine biologists should always use scientific names, says Arthur. Not to use the scientific name, he says, "reflects badly on you as a scientist."

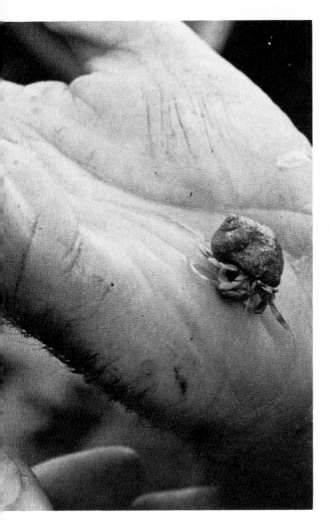

The next spadeful of mud produces two of Arthur's favorite invertebrates, *Pagurus longicarpus* (Puh-GYOO-rus lon-ji-KAR-pus), the hermit crab, and *Pectinaria gouldi* (Peck-ti-NAR-ee-uh GOOLD-eye), the trumpet worm. Each lacks protective armor, so each has found its own ingenious way of protecting itself. The hermit crab, *Pagurus*, lives in empty snail shells and holds itself in place by means of rough spots on its tail and rear legs. In fact, its name, *Pagurus longicarpus*, literally means "that which fastens itself by its long legs."

By contrast, *Pectinaria*, or trumpet worm, lives in the mud in a tube which it cements for itself using thousands of tiny sand grains. Both these animals are common in muddy areas, but, as Arthur says, they're always delightful to find.

While Arthur and his group search the water, Tom Duncan and some others explore a patch of drier mud riddled with strange nickel-sized holes. What made the holes? Using a clamrake Tom gently scrapes the mud, and suddenly, snapping and scrambling sideways from one of the holes, comes a *Uca* (YOU-kuh), or fiddler crab.

There are three species of *Ucas*, Tom tells the students: *Uca pugilator* (pyou-ji-LAY-tor), which tends to live in sandy areas; *Uca minax* (MIN-aks), which burrows in ground above water; and *Uca pugnax* (PUG-naks), like this one, which burrows in intertidal mud. Tom knows this one's a male because one claw is bigger than the other. Tom says not to worry about their claws — they don't hurt when they pinch. But making a *Uca* stand still in your hands can be a problem.

Up along the marshy part of the cove Arthur finds some old boards washed there by storms and high tides. They're easy places to miss but if you overturn some you're likely to find a few marsh snails, *Melampus bidentatus* (muh-LAM-pus bee-den-TAH-tus).

Melampus lives under such debris for moisture and protection from the sun. But in addition, the boards crush the marsh grass underneath them, causing it to decay, and decaying marsh grass, as Arthur explains, is *Melampus*'s favorite food.

 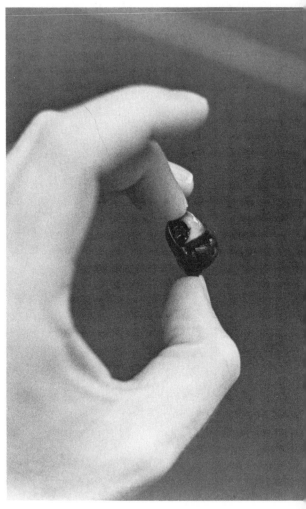

Other snails, such as the common periwinkle, *Littorina littorea* (lit-toe-RYE-nuh lit-toe-REE-uh), prefer eating simpler plants called *algae* (AL-jee). So instead of hiding under boards, *Littorina* lives along the shore, on rocks, where many algae grow.

 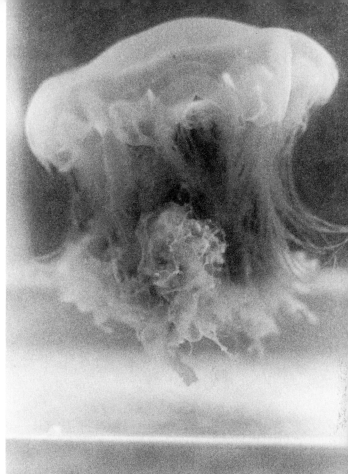

Arthur and Tom are poking through the shore grass when they come upon a dead jellyfish, *Cyanea capillata* (cy-A-nee-uh cap-li-LA-tuh), known commonly as a red, or lion's mane jellyfish. Arthur picks it up. Normally, if the *Cyanea* were alive, Arthur's hands would be stung by the creature's long tentacles. But now, dead, the tentacles are harmless, mere strings dangling from the *Cyanea*'s sloppy corpse.

Alive, a *Cyanea* is a beautiful creature with a domed brownish pink bell and fluttering lip-shaped edges called *lappets*. *Cyanea* are *planktonic*, which means they hardly swim, but instead drift with the ocean currents. They're the largest species of jellyfish in the world, and some attain sizes up to eight feet across, though most are much smaller.

Arthur's class once captured a *Cyanea* about ten inches across. In the laboratory sea tank its tentacles pulsed and wavered like silken threads. The class studied it admiringly for a day, then released it.

Field trips like this one are scheduled for low tide because that is when the intertidal zones are exposed. Arthur has timed this field trip perfectly. While the class has been working along shore, the water in the cove has been draining into the sea. The tide finally reaches dead low. Now the class can cross the mud to the cove's sandy intertidal zone.

And there, you just sink a spade into the wet sand, and all kinds of wonderful creatures pop forth.

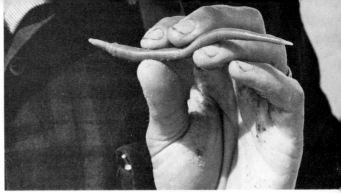

There are razor clams. Scientifically known as *Ensis directus* (EN-sis duh-REC-tus), or "one shaped like a straight sword," these clams burrow deep into the intertidal sand. In fact, says Arthur, when you find one, it will likely try to burrow away from you, but a quick plunge of the shovel can cut off its retreat.

Another burrowing creature is the worm called *Phascolopsis gouldi* (Fass-co-LOP-sis GOOLD-eye), a long, rubbery, pencil-shaped creature that can retract the front part of its body back into itself. Such worms feed on various wastes, either in the water or the sand, and thus play an important role in cleaning their environment.

On the surface of the sand, among some weeds, Arthur finds a bay scallop, *Aequipecten irradians* (Ee-kwi-PECK-tin ear-RAY-dee-enz). Like the *Mercenaria* clam found earlier, *Aequipecten* is a *bivalve*, which means it has two openings, one for sucking water in (along with food and oxygen), and the other for blowing water out (along with wastes). In water, this scallop opens his shell, revealing a double row of blue *ocelli* (OSS-uh-lye), or eyes, with which the scallop senses light and movements.

To catch any swimming invertebrates, Arthur has some students drag the water with a long, fine-meshed nylon net called a *bait seine*.

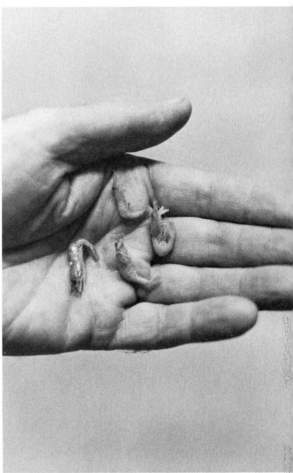

Mostly the bait seine snags seaweed. But if you look closely among the weeds, says Arthur, you'll usually find some shore shrimp, *Palaemontes vulgaris* (Puh-lee-mow-NEE-tees VUL-guhr-is). Known commercially as a prawn, *Palaemontes* swims using its middle feet, called *pleopods* (PLEE-oh-pods), but when in danger it can dart backwards with a powerful jackknifing kick of its body.

Soon it is time to leave. The tide is beginning to rise and in an hour the little cove will again be submerged in water. Smiles warm the air. The collecting buckets are full. Altogether the class has found some sixty different species of marine invertebrates.

"How was the cove?" Captain Lane asks when the group arrives at the pier.

"Nice," smiles one of the female students.

"Muddy!" shouts a male student.

"Well, come aboard anyway," says Captain Lane. And the students all clamber aboard the ship.

As the *Ciona* quits the harbor and the island shrinks from view, Arthur glances at his students, most of them quiet, and thinks, They were good. They worked hard. Jacques Loeb, Louis Agassiz — all the greats in the field began this way.

The thought that the students may have both learned from the trip and enjoyed it gives the teacher in Arthur a small sense of joy.

In his mind he can already see them as full-fledged marine scientists.

The return passage to Woods Hole is calm.

Island coves aren't the only places studied by marine biologists. Other intertidal sites abound on Cape Cod, and Arthur wants his students to know the invertebrate species in each.

One day, using BUMP's tan truck and blue van, the class drives to Nobska Point on the southern tip of Woods Hole.

Besides being the site of a working Coast Guard lighthouse, Nobska Point is a perfect example of a rocky intertidal zone.

In fact, says Arthur, each rock in such an area is itself an intertidal zone, encrusted as it is with living forms. Look closely, he says, and you'll see that plants and animals attach themselves to the rocks in belts, or bands, with each band representing a different species. For example, across the middle of an intertidal rock you'll always find a whitish band of *Balanus* (BAL-uh-nus), or acorn barnacles as they're commonly called. Arthur says that *Balanus* bands are an easy way to tell the tide levels because the top edge of the band is always at the high tide mark.

Balanus is not so easy to collect, though. Its hard base squirts a limy glue that sticks it firmly to any solid intertidal surface. Arthur either scrapes a specimen off the rock using a jack-knife, or chips it free with hammer and chisel.

On the underside of the rock, below water, you can usually find different *Porifera* (Por-IF-er-uh), which are simple invertebrates that most of us know as sponges.

If you search hard you'll always find an *Asterias* (Ass-TARE-ee-us), or sea star.

Arthur says, for short-term study, the best way to keep these animals alive is in containers filled with seawater.

Most marine biologists know snorkeling and scuba diving so they can study marine creatures in their natural homes, or *habitats* as they're scientifically called. Mas Dojiri takes groups of students snorkeling off the Nobska Point rocks. On any dive they're likely to find:

Lobster (*Homarus americanus*)
(Ho-MAR-us uh-mer-i-KAHN-us)

Homarus is a slow grower, needing four years to reach weights of 1 ½ to 2 pounds. Besides its long, whiplike antennae, used for touching, *Homarus* has hundreds of taste and touch receptors on its walking legs and mouth parts, and smell receptors on its two smaller antennae, known to marine biologists as *antennules*.

Purple sea urchin (*Arabacia punctulata*)
(Ar-uh-BAY-cee-uh punk-tu-LA-ta)

You can always tell an *Arabacia* by its purplish color and its beautiful, though prickly, movable spines. An *Arabacia's* skeleton is called a *test*, and if you study it closely, you'll see that it's actually composed of numerous closely fitting shell-like plates.

Sea pork (*Amaroucium stellatum*)
(Am-uh-ROO-see-um stel-LA-tum)

Can you believe that this weird, pink, rubbery stuff is actually a colony of animals? It is, and like clams and sponges, the animals feed by filtering seawater through their bodies. In turn, sharks, sting rays, and other bottom feeders eat them.

Sea spider (*Pycnogonum littorale*)
(pick-no-GO-num lit-toe-RAL-ee)

Sea spiders are different from land spiders. For one, their bodies are one-instead of two-parted, and for another, sea spiders can't spin webs. Little is known about what sea spiders eat, and they're hard to catch, except with an extremely fine meshed net.

Most people think you can't find anything on sandy beaches except seashells. But good marine biologists know that if they dig down a few feet near the water they'll find mole crabs, *Emerita talpoida* (Em-uh-REE-tuh tal-poy-EE-duh), which are harmless creatures whose ten legs and egg-shaped shells are perfectly fashioned for burrowing.

And when sand samples are taken from different depths along the shoreline and examined under a microscope, the beach's chief residents appear.

They are worms called *Nematoda* (nee-muh-TOE-duh), which in Latin means "thread-shaped." Nematodes live by the billions in beaches throughout the world. In fact, just two cubic feet of beach sand can contain over one million nematodes.

The same sand can also contain thousands of sand lice, or *Harpactacoid copepods* (har-PACK-tuh-koyd KO-puh-pods). This is a *Harpactacoid* that Arthur found in sand from a Woods Hole beach. Under the microscope the sand grains look like boulders.

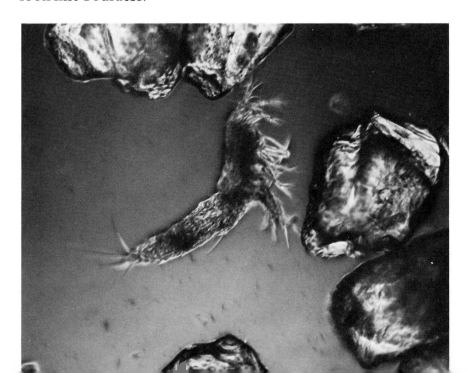

Enough marine animals live along the shore to give a marine biologist a lifetime's worth of things to study. But good marine biologists should know the animals of the oceans, too. Arthur Humes and his students study the marine invertebrates in the waters off Cape Cod from strong ships like the *Super Horse*, a 65-foot fishing vessel that docks in Woods Hole.

Each of the ship voyages lasts a full day, and as leader of the expeditions Arthur is the *chief scientist* on board. The principal tool used for collecting specimens from the ocean floor is a *dredge*, whose heavy iron mouth scrapes along the bottom, pushing animals into its thick burlap bag. An engine-powered wheel called a *winch* lowers the dredge to the bottom on a long steel cable.

A single dredging usually takes five minutes. Then the winch hauls up the dredge and the contents of its bag are dumped on the ship's deck. The students then sort out the specimens at the ship's rail on a special platform called a *sea table*.

Sea specimens are often exotic and beautiful. At one spot in Cape Cod Bay called Fishing Ledge, Arthur always dredges up a basket star, which has the tongue-twisting scientific name *Gorgonocephalus arcticus* (Gor-gon-o-SEFF-uh-lus ARK-tick-us). In Greek mythology the Gorgons were three sisters with snakes for hair. In Latin, *Gorgonocephalus* means "one with a head like a Gorgon." It's one of Arthur's favorite specimens.

Another is the sand dollar (*Echinarachhius parma*, eh-kine-uh-ROCK-ee-us PAR-muh), which is neither a dollar nor made of sand, but rather an invertebrate animal covered with soft, velvetlike spines that help it move over sandy ocean bottoms. Alive, most sand dollars appear brownish, splotched with red and purple, but dead they turn pale white and are brittle to the touch. Arthur and his class once caught hundreds of sand dollars in a single dredging north of the Cape Cod Canal. They took only three specimens, pushing the rest back into the sea.

The *plankton net* is another essential tool on any research ship, and Arthur always brings one with him when he and his students go to sea. Towed behind the ship on a rope, the net skims just below the ocean surface, collecting the floating plant and animal life called *plankton* (PLANK-tun) in its path.

Most plankton are tiny, less than one-eighth inch long. But marine biologists will tell you how important plankton are as food for many whales and fishes. "Without plankton there would be no fish," says Arthur, "and conceivably without fish there would be no man." In fact, plankton are so important that there's a whole branch of marine biology devoted exclusively to plankton study called *planktology*.

Field trips, whether one day or longer, comprise only part of a marine biologist's working life. The rest of the time is spent in the laboratory, doing experiments, studying specimens, and writing scientific reports. When Arthur Humes and his class return from a field trip, they know they have their work cut out for them. Now, returning from their island voyage, Arthur and the marine students unload the bucketfuls of specimens from the ship and carry them up to a special room on the second floor of the Loeb building. It's time to leave the outdoors for a while and go to work in the laboratory.

In 210 Loeb, which is the laboratory where first-year BUMP students work, specimens collected on the trip are transferred to waiting tanks filled with running seawater. The tanks, like the collecting buckets, are numbered, and a record has been kept of where each bucketful of specimens was collected on the island.

Each student is responsible for identifying the animals in one tank, and they do this by examining the animals — sometimes under microscopes — and comparing what they see with special reference guides called *keys*.

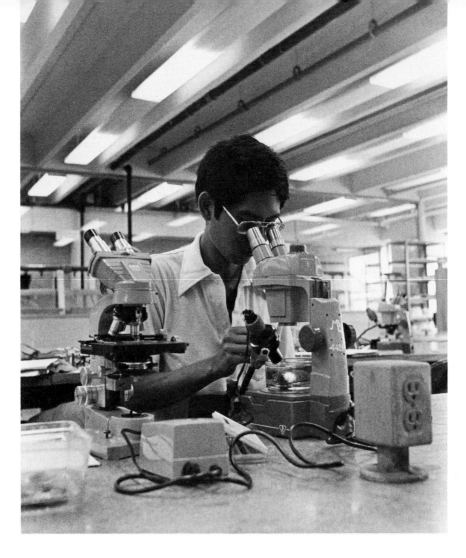

Microscopes are important tools to marine biologists. Often invertebrate animals are small, or look so much alike that it's impossible to tell one from another with the naked eye. But under the microscope all these differences come clear.

For the rest of the afternoon, Arthur's students study the day's specimens. Usually Arthur stops by the lab and helps identify a few of the animals. But then he leaves, because if the students ever hope to become good marine biologists they must learn to do scientific work on their own. Arthur returns to his office where his own scientific work is waiting.

Good marine biologists must be able to work alone, says Arthur, because that is how most scientific research gets done. To earn a Ph.D. from BUMP, every student must complete an independent research project in his or her favorite branch of marine biology. There are two kinds of scientific research: *pure research*, which opens new knowledge in a certain area; and *applied research*, which tries to solve specific problems facing us all.

Most BUMP students' projects are a blend of each. For example, Cabell Davis, one of BUMP's advanced students, is interested in the fish we eat and what controls their populations. So, for three years he has studied *zoöplankton* (ZOO-oh-plank-tun), the basic food for most fish. By measuring the abundance of zoöplankton in a given place, he says, you can begin to estimate the size of the fish population, and thus set accurate limits on how many fish can be caught there.

Concentrated on Georges Bank, a major fishing ground off the New England coast, Cabell's research took him on many voyages aboard the *Albatross IV*, a 187-foot research vessel owned by the National Marine Fisheries Service. Cabell sampled the waters for zoöplankton using a variety of plankton nets, some of whose tows he tracked on the ship's radar scope.

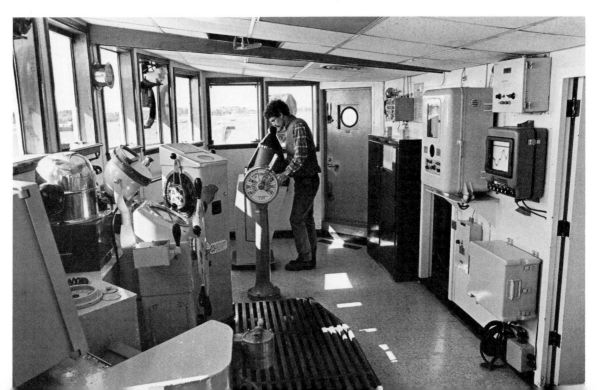

Sometimes marine biologists' talents take them to far-off places. As a marine taxonomist, BUMP student Isabelle Williams is skilled in handling all sorts of marine invertebrate animals. So when the Woods Hole Oceanographic Institution organized an expedition to the famed Galapagos Rift Vents near the Galapagos Islands, Isabelle was hired as one of the *curators* responsible for organizing and keeping records about the invertebrates collected on the voyage.

The vents, discovered in 1977, are warm-water openings in the earth's crust lying two miles below the ocean's surface. Most important, they are a breeding ground for numerous exotic creatures. To collect some of these, the expedition team used *Alvin*, a miniature three-man submarine with specially built collecting claws on its prow. Isabelle and others waited aboard *Lulu, Alvin*'s mother ship. When a fresh collection of specimens came aboard, the curators went to work, labeling and preserving them for future study.

Isabelle's chief responsibility were the mussels that *Alvin* collected. "It was very exciting," she says. "The dives brought up species nobody had ever seen before. And for me it was personally exciting visiting a different part of the world. The only sad thing happened in Costa Rica: my camera was stolen."

BUMP student Russell Hill's interests range from photography to electronics, so what better way of doing both as a marine biologist than by specializing in *neurobiology*, the study of animals' nervous systems. Russell became fascinated in how lobsters open and close their big claws, which is a question more complicated than it sounds. For example, the claws encased in shell are still very sensitive. "Just blowing through a claw can cause it to snap shut," Russell says.

By using an *oscilloscope*, an instrument which, when wired to a lobster claw, translates nerve energy into visual signals, Russell could watch the firing pattern along the animal's nerves. "A lobster has three types of nerves," he says; "one that carries signals to open the claw, another that carries signals to close it, and a third that carries signals to keep it shut. Each of these nerves works in a different way."

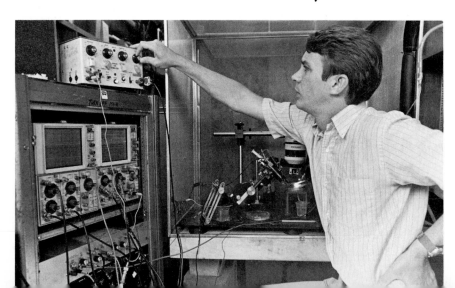

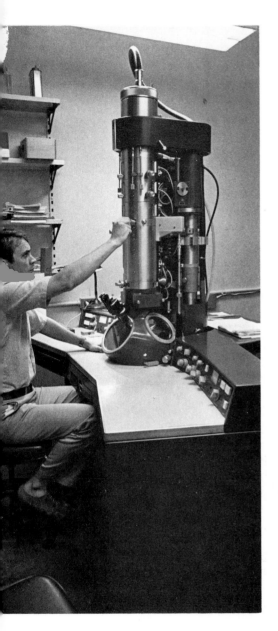

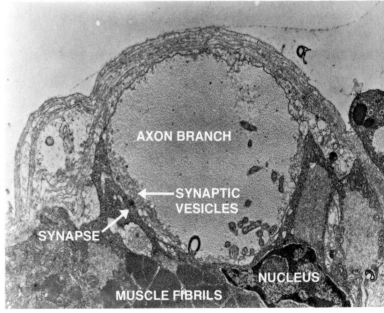

Later, using an electron microscope, Russell photographed cross sections of the nerves and muscles to see what each nerve looked like. This is one of his photos of an *axon*, a place on the nerve where signals to open and close are actually passed to the claw muscles. Axons are tiny. Thanks to the electron microscope this cross section has been magnified 14,000 times. But understanding how this lobster axon works, says Russell, can help us understand the human nervous system. In fact, he and others think it may even help us understand such crippling diseases as muscular distrophy.

Lobsters aren't the only animals whose senses interest BUMP students. Bruce Bryant studies catfish because of their extraordinary senses of taste and smell. "Catfish smell with their noses and taste with their mouths," says Bruce, "but taste buds cover their face barbels and the rest of their bodies, too. In addition, they can sense water vibrations and electric fields that other fish produce."

Bruce's teacher, Jelle (YELL-uh) Atema, got Bruce wondering why catfish need so many sense organs. By observing the effects of different odors on pairs of catfish, and by recording those observations on a tape recorder and later on a computer, Bruce and others have found that catfish rely on smell and taste in ways that other animals depend on eyesight.

Such *behavioral study* as Bruce's helps biologists in many fields understand the ways in which sense mechanisms serve animals.

Sometimes pollution or other factors can change an animal's sense mechanisms. Tom Trott, another BUMP behavioral student, is studying the effects of offshore oil drilling on lobsters. Scientists already know that lobsters and other marine creatures can sicken or actually die from oil spilled in the sea. But now Tom and others are finding that just the chemical drilling mud used for forcing oil from underground may also have harmful effects on lobsters. In a BUMP lab Tom studies the burrowing behavior of four-month-old baby lobsters. Those lobsters in the tanks without drilling mud dig perfect burrows, as is normal for their age. But those in the tanks with drilling mud run frantically around or try to swim up the tank. In early experiments, some baby lobsters that came in contact with the mud got sick, but it's too early to tell just how harmful different drilling muds are.

Dr. Atema, who oversees these experiments, says it's a scientist's duty to give information that will help us make right decisions about environmental questions. "And yet," he says, "as a scientist I don't feel I have any special answers into how to conduct our future."

Arthur agrees and adds, "If we could tell the future, we probably wouldn't be scientists, we'd be fortune tellers or politicians."

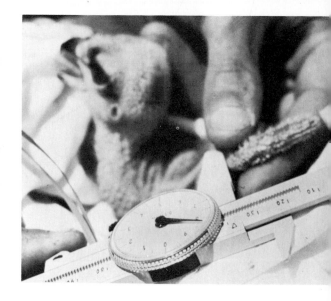

Alan Poole is neither of these. A BUMP student who loves birds, Alan is a *marine ornithologist* whose chief area of research is ospreys. As recently as 1971 the osprey population along the Atlantic Coast was decreasing because of harmful amounts of the pesticide DDT in the fish they ate. But since a federal ban on DDT in 1972, ospreys have been making a comeback, and now Alan wants to know what else might limit their population.

For the past three years he has studied the three hundred or so ospreys that nest coastally between New York and Boston. Since food supply can limit a population, Alan keeps track of what the ospreys eat by watching them through telescopes, visiting their nests, and combing the ground below their nests for bones.

Alan enjoys weighing and measuring the birds the most. "The traps we catch them with don't hurt the birds," he says. "The dome trap, for example, with its nylon loops for snaring a female osprey by her talons, is harmless. So are the hoods, which quiet the birds. And the minute we finish our measurings, the osprey is released."

Alan once taught high school English for a living, but says now he's doing what he loves the most.

So is Jean Hartman. For a time she thought she was going to be a computer engineer, until a backpacking trip to Alaska convinced her otherwise. She discovered she liked wild plants and flowers, wanted to learn more about them, wanted to make plant study, or *botany*, her life work. So now she is a marine botanist doing doctoral work on three species of marsh plant called *Salicornia* (Sal-uh-CORN-ee-uh).

"I'm interested in succession," she says, "in how new plant species replace older ones. *Salicornia* is usually the first plant to take hold in a bare marshy spot, so by studying it, I also study the whole pattern of plant life in the marsh."

Nina Caraco studies patterns, too, but her realm of interest is a coastal salt pond in a residential part of Cape Cod. "I first became interested in why so much algae glutted the pond," she says. "Were the fertilizers washing down from the lawns feeding the algae? Or the salt water that drains in from the sea? Or the droppings from migratory birds?"

Nina's questions led her to a year-round study of the pond's waters. A report she co-authored has already helped officials decide what to do about the algae problem, and before she's through, the pond may become one of the most researched bodies of water in New England.

Even now the Great Sippewissett Marsh, which is north of Woods Hole, is the most researched marsh in the world. For the past ten years BUMP professor Ivan Valiela has been studying how the soil, air, water, and living forms of the marsh act on each other. Such study of biological communities is called *ecology*, and Dr. Valiela and the students who work with him are marine ecologists.

One of Dr. Valiela's ongoing experiments involves the effects of sludge pollutants on the marsh. The sludge, which is dried and sterilized waste from sewage treatment centers, is scattered on plots in different amounts, and tests are run year round to check the effects. Does the sludge hurt the marsh? Dr. Valiela doesn't think so. "The pollutants in the sludge tend not to wash away," he says, "and the marsh seems to make the sludge less poisonous." Results so far suggest that the marsh might make a good *tertiary treatment*, or final dumping site for waste in this form.

Besides pollutants, Dr. Valiela and his students want to know how *nutrients* affect marsh life. So, at a place called the *biostimulation site* liquid fertilizer containing certain nutrients is sprayed on the marsh for a set period each day.

The fertilizer is pumped by means of a diesel engine which is housed near the site in a metal hut called a van.

Periodically, teams of students and technicians take various measurements at the fertilized and unfertilized sites to compare them.

Brian Howes, a fifth-year BUMP student, analyzes the soil and water on the sites with the aid of such instruments as this probe which measures oxygen and acids in the soil.

Using a special tool called a core sampler, BUMP student Ken Foreman extracts samples of marsh mud to study the effects of fertilization on the *meiofauna* (MY-oh-faw-nuh), or small animals that live there.

And Dr. Valiela reviews all the information or data about the marsh, and leads in the work of organizing and analyzing it.

As one student said, "The marsh is a beautiful place, and the more you study one part of it, the more you see how that connects with every other part, which is what ecology is all about in the first place."

And what about Arthur Humes and his taxonomic work? Over the past thirty years he has discovered some four hundred new species of animals called *copepods* (KO-puh-pods), a name which comes from the Greek words *copa*, meaning *oar*, and *poda*, meaning *feet*. Copepods are tiny flea- or shrimplike animals whose size can range anywhere from several millimeters (a fraction of an inch) down to 300 microns (as small as the smallest dust speck). And yet these tiny creatures intrigue Arthur Humes because of the different ways they live beneath the sea. Many copepods are *parasites*, living and feeding on fish and other animals. Other copepods are planktonic, floating wherever the ocean currents take them. Fish eat these copepods, and humans eat fish, so it's safe to say that copepods form one of the first and most important links in the food chain.

Dr. Humes has searched for copepods all over the world. His discoveries of new copepods and their relation to other animals are important because they help science better understand the ocean as an *ecosystem*, that is, a vast community of life.

The species he is studying today came from this piece of coral which he collected while scuba diving near an island off Madagascar called Nosy Bé.

The copepods live on the surface of the coral and in the craterlike hollows called *cups*.

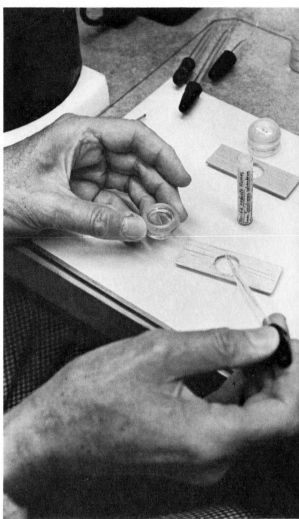

To remove the copepods for study without squashing them, Arthur soaked the coral in a solution of ethyl alcohol and water. The alcohol made the copepods drunk; they released themselves from the coral, and Arthur was able to collect them by straining the solution through extremely fine mesh.

Now he takes a small vial containing three or four copepods out of its storage jar. The vial contains a stronger alcohol solution, which has killed the copepods but preserved them intact.

The copepods are transferred for study to a microscope slide by means of a tapered glass tube with a rubber bulb at one end called a *pipette*. Next comes a drop of lactic acid, which *clears* the specimen — that is, makes it easier to see.

 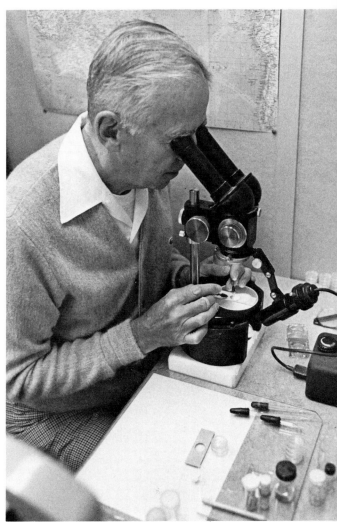

Then, to study the structure, or *anatomy*, of the copepod, Arthur takes a special tungsten needle in either hand, and peering through his microscope he begins cutting the copepod into its basic parts. Such systematic cutting of a specimen is called a *dissection*, and it takes steady hands and a great deal of patience to do this one right.

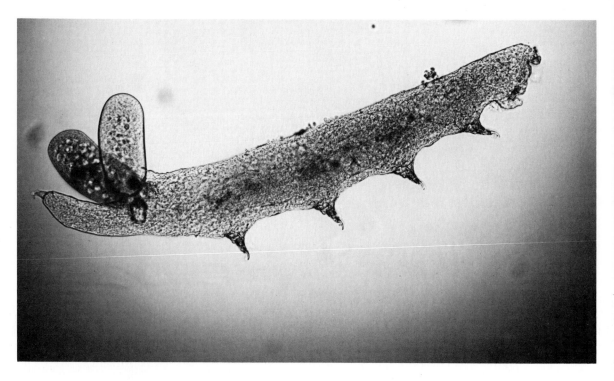

Arthur always pauses just to look at a specimen before beginning a dissection. This copepod resembles a stubby ten-
legged worm. If you look closely, says Arthur, you can see
the tiny hooklike leg endings which help the copepod cling to
the coral cups.

And its sex? "It's a female. See the egg sacs?" says Arthur.

Not all copepods look like this one. Most of the planktonic
ones have longer legs. And some that are parasites on fishes
look like miniature prehistoric monsters.

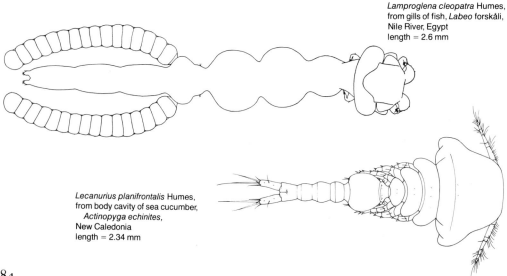

Lamproglena cleopatra Humes,
from gills of fish, *Labeo* forskåli,
Nile River, Egypt
length = 2.6 mm

Lecanurius planifrontalis Humes,
from body cavity of sea cucumber,
  Actinopyga echinites,
New Caledonia
length = 2.34 mm

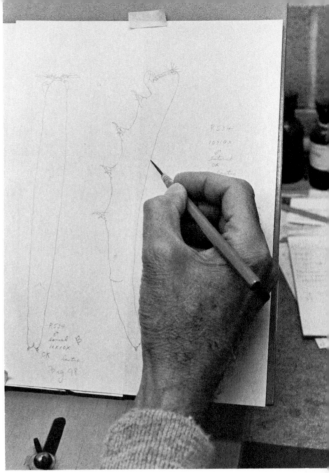

Working carefully and steadily, Arthur dissects the copepod. His eyes are relaxed. The needles feel like extensions of his fingers. Since no one else has seen this species of copepod before, Arthur will make its existence known to the world by publishing a paper about it in one of the many scientific magazines that scientists read, called journals. But first he needs illustrations of the animal. How do you draw pictures of something that's microscopic? By means of a beautiful instrument called a *camera lucida*, which clamps to the side of the microscope. How does it work? A carefully angled system of prisms and mirrors shows Arthur the reflection of his own hand and the drawing board to the right. But at the same time the microscope shows him the image of the copepod. The two images — of the copepod, and the drawing board and his hand — seem sandwiched one atop the other. Amazing as it seems, Arthur can look through the microscope and trace the exact outline of the copepod onto the drawing paper!

Later, he will give the tracings to an artist who lives near Woods Hole. She in turn will ink the drawings using waterproof black India ink and a variety of fine-pointed pens.

When the inked drawings return from the artist, Arthur mounts and labels them for publication on special-sized pieces of white cardboard. This is the fun part of a marine taxonomist's work, and the finished drawings always look exquisite.

The hard part is writing the scientific paper, which any scientist will tell you must be clear, concise, and accurate. Before a marine biologist begins writing — about an experiment, or a new species, or a scientific study — he first does what scientists call a *literature search*. That means he must review all the existing scientific papers relating to his subject to be sure, among other things, that he hasn't duplicated anyone else's work.

Arthur does his search at the Marine Biological Laboratory library, which has copies of practically every important scientific journal published in the world. Not all are written in English, though. "As a marine biologist you must know either Russian, French, or German," says Arthur, "because those are the other languages in which most scientific journals are written."

Once the literature search is done, Arthur writes his paper. The first draft comes quickly, but he rewrites that at least four or five times. Arthur describes all the key features of the new copepod species, as well as when and where he discovered it. And as its discoverer, he gives the copepod a name. "*Xarifia* [zuh-RIFF-ee-uh] is the name of this species," says Arthur, "after the German research vessel *Xarifa* whose scientists sent me specimens of the copepod from one of their expeditions."

It is late afternoon. Arthur is reviewing the first draft of his paper on *Xarifia* when Dorothy Hahn knocks on his office door. "This just came by special delivery," she says, handing him a letter. It's from the National Science Foundation in Washington, D.C. "Dear Dr. Humes," it reads, "We are delighted to inform you that your research grant has been approved. . . ." It names him the recipient of eighty thousand dollars, enough money for him to continue his copepod research over the next three years.

"Mas," Arthur telephones Mas Dojiri in his office, "can you come in here a moment? I've got good news." For Mas, the letter means that he can be Arthur's part-time research assistant, his salary paid for by money from Arthur's grant. For Arthur, it means he can travel to Panama and Hawaii, in part to see if *Xarifia* and its cousins live that far east.

"Fantastic!" whispers Mas Dojiri.

"Congratulations," says Dorothy Hahn.

Research grants are the chief means by which scientific work is funded, and the National Science Foundation awards many grants. Now, eighty thousand dollars may sound like a lot of money, but from it Arthur must budget his research expenses over the next three years. And those expenses include equipment, travel expenses, a salary for Mas, publication and drawing costs for the scientific papers he will write, and many, many more. "It's a generous grant," says Arthur, "but I can't just spend it on anything."

Nevertheless, at six o'clock when he walks upstairs to his students' lab, he is smiling.

In the lab a celebration is in progress. Today is Tom Duncan's birthday. Someone has made a beef stew for the occasion, and others have brought bread, wine, salad, butter, and three nice carrot cakes with lemon vanilla frosting.

The supper also welcomes Howard Sanders, a scientist from the Woods Hole Oceanographic Institution and a long-time friend of Arthur's, who tonight will lecture the students on the diversity of animals in the deep-sea.

Lectures by guest scientists are a regular part of Arthur's course in marine zoology, and Dr. Sanders is one of the world's foremost authorities in his field.

Arthur's marine zoology course runs for a total of six weeks, and when it's over he hopes to spend more time on his own research.

Meanwhile, the next field trip — to Nantucket Sound this time — is scheduled for the day after tomorrow. And come the end of the term there are student lectures to hear and research papers to correct: projects given the students to help them become good marine biologists.

At 9 P.M., after Dr. Sanders' lecture and fourteen hours after he came to work, Arthur can lock his office door and go home for the night.

There is so much to know. The beautiful truth about marine biology, Arthur Humes will tell you, is that no matter what branch you choose — and there are dozens — your life will be an endless quest. "There is always another question, another mystery drawing you onward," he says, "and an excitement that goes with the search." For Arthur Humes that search began on a beach as a little boy. It still continues — touching Panama, Hawaii, every part of the globe.

Man is a creature of land, says Arthur, yet his curiosity is boundless. As long as the sea remains, man's passion for new knowledge about its life will remain, too.

APPENDIX

Marine biology is a profession with many specialized branches. Below is a list of the major areas of marine biology and their definitions:

marine zoology: the study of invertebrates and vertebrates (animals with backbones) in the sea. Specialties include *marine mammalogy*, the study of marine mammals, such as whales and manatees; *ichthyology*, the study of fishes; *parasitology*, the study of marine parasites; *invertebrate zoology*, the study of marine invertebrates, and dozens more.

marine algology: the study of the simple marine plants known as algae.

marine ecology: the study of the relationships between marine plants and animals and their environments.

marine physiology: the study of the structure and function of the cells, tissues, and organs of marine plants and animals.

marine behaviorism: the study of marine animal and plant behavior under both natural and laboratory conditions.

marine biochemistry: the study of the chemical composition and chemical processes of plants and animals in the sea.

marine bacteriology: the study of bacteria in the sea and how they relate to other marine life.

fisheries biology: the study of fish populations for purposes of regulating commercial fishing.

aquaculture biology: the use of biological information for purposes of fish and marine plant farming.

For those readers interested in learning more about marine biology as a profession, I recommend Dr. Humes's article, "Marine Biology as a Career" in *The American Biology Teacher*, Volume 40, Number 3 (March 1978).

ACKNOWLEDGMENTS

I wish to thank the staff and students of the Boston University Marine Program for all their help and cooperation during my work on this book.

I would also like to thank the Marine Biological Laboratory, Woods Hole, Massachusetts; the National Marine Fisheries Service, Woods Hole; and the Woods Hole Oceanographic Institution for letting me photograph in and around their buildings and ships.

For their very special contributions to this book, my particular thanks goes to Sarah Allen, Lieutenant Commander A. Y. Bryson, William Clench, Carmela Cuomo, Charles Derby, Masahiro Dojiri, Dr. Thomas Duncan, William Fahey, James Fones, Anne Giblin, Dale Goehringer, Nancy Green, Dorothy Hahn, Robin Harrington, Brian Howes, Captain "Brud" Lane, William Lange, Anthony and Ann Moss, Alan Poole, Mary Porter, Dr. Howard Sanders, Dr. Sidney Tamm, Dr. Ruth Turner, Richard Van Etten, and Michael Yamin. And for their presence on this trip, my love and thanks to Pam, Andrew, and Petya Rostova.

My gratitude, as always, goes to Ward Rice of The Camera Store, Stowe, Vermont, who printed the photographs for this book, and without whom I couldn't imagine tackling any *Day in the Life* at all.

Finally, my great good thanks to Dr. Arthur Humes, a dedicated scientist and teacher, and wonderful, generous man, for so cheerfully lending his reality to this layman's dream.

Blessings upon you all!

W J